The Gender Link
to the Human Soul

Kimberly Bruce

En Route Books and Media, LLC

Saint Louis, MO

⊕*ENROUTE*
Make the time

En Route Books and Media, LLC
5705 Rhodes Avenue
St. Louis, MO 63109

contactus@enroutebooksandmedia.com

Cover credit: Sebastian Mahfood and Gustav
Doré
Copyright © 2022 Kimberly Bruce

ISBN-13: 978-1-956715-23-1
Library of Congress Control Number
2022930795

Table of Contents

INTRODUCTION

"Gender" is a term with a varied meaning today in contrast with the usage of this
term barely three decades ago.[1] Prior to the
1990's, gender was almost exclusively understood as pertaining to one's natural-born
biological sex (male or female);[2] however, it

---

[1] In 1985, Taber's Cyclopedic Medical Dic-
tionary defined "gender" as "the sex of an indi-
vidual, i.e, male or female." Clarence Wilbur
Tabor, "Gender," in *Tabor's Cyclopedic Medical
Dictionary*, ed. Clayton L. Thomas (Philadelphia,
PA: F.A. Davis Company, 1985), 671.

[2] An historical review of human rights from
the 1990's pertaining to international law
acknowledges common usage of the term "gender" in identifying one as male or female while
simultaneously rejecting a "radical re-definition
of *gender* as a social construct to promote a sexually polymorphous view of the human person."
Jane Adolphe and Robert L. Fastiggi, "Gender

1

has since taken on a different connotation in the United States and around the world to be the *subjective* gender with which one identifies oneself.[3] In light of society's present-day preoccupation with gender, one may wonder to what extent gender really matters in this life, *or*, is it so integrally connected to the human person that it is not only important in the here and now, but retained as part of our personhood in the afterlife as well—as part of our eternal *souls*?

Identifying gender as being an everlasting attribute of one's eternal soul distinguishes gender as being fundamental and intrinsic to the human person—a quality that is *retained*—not shed, "done away with"

(in International Law)," in *New Catholic Encyclopedia Supplement 2012-2013: Ethics and Philosophy*, vol. 2, ed. Robert L. Fastiggi (Detroit: Gale, 2013), 612.

[3] Scott Stiegemeyer, "How Do You Know Whether You are a Man or a Woman?" *Concordia Theological Quarterly* 79, no. 1-2 (2015): 23.

nor morphed into its opposite in the life to come. There are some philosophers, searching for what is essential and non-essential to human nature, who consider gender "a social construct" able to be "changed at will."[4] Gender as a malleable social construct, however, proves untenable in the light of Catholic teaching, the Bible, and the writings of many declared saints. This book will provide an in-depth look at the relationship between gender and one's eternal soul by first defining "gender" and the "soul"; looking at physical and chemical determinants of gender; exploring gender abnormalities; considering gender difference; and describing what the Bible and the Catholic Church teach about gender—particularly through the writings of John Paul II and Thomas Aquinas, and as

---

[4] J. Marianne Siegmund. "Gender: Philosophy of," in *New Catholic Encyclopedia Supplement 2012-2013: Ethics and Philosophy*, vol. 2, ed. Robert L. Fastiggi (Detroit: Gale, 2013), 614.

evidenced by Christ's own Resurrection and Ascension into Heaven.

Disseminating truth about gender is of paramount importance to a world steeped in a myriad of understandings of what it means to be male and female, to a world immersed in growing acceptance that gender is irrelevant and malleable, and to a world that increasingly believes gender is not a permanent quality of a person maintained in the afterlife. John Paul II's *Man and Woman He Created Them: A Theology of the Body* and Thomas Aquinas's *Summa Theologiae* are very articulate and powerful in making the case for gender's existence in the afterlife and are heavily referenced in the coming chapters, as are many other quotes from saints, philosophers, and theologians supporting the expressions of these spiritual giants.

CHAPTER 1

GENDER AND THE SOUL

GENDER DEFINED

Until recent times, the terms "gender" and "sex" were used interchangeably to denote an individual as being either a male or female.[1] The term "sex" is still regularly used to indicate one as being male or female, but "gender," as previously mentioned, is often now used to convey one's "subjective internal sense" of being a male, female, or both (transgender).[2] The Oxford English Dictionary defines "gender" as either, a) "Males or females viewed as a group," and "the property or fact of belonging to one of these

---

[1] Scott Stiegemeyer, "How Do You Know Whether You are a Man or a Woman?" *Concordia Theological Quarterly* 79, no. 1-2 (2015): 23.

[2] Stiegemeyer, 23.

groups," but provides, as well, a psychological and sociological definition, which is b) "The state of being male or female as expressed by social or cultural distinctions and differences, rather than biological ones."[3] The definition of "gender" found in Tabor's Cyclopedic Medical Dictionary, however, as being "the sex of an individual, i.e., male or female,"[4] is the most accurate definition for "gender" used for the purposes of gender discussion contained within this book.

In the very first chapter of the Bible, God says, "'Let us make humankind in our image, according to our likeness'...So God created humankind in his image, in the image of God he created them; male and female he created them. God blessed them, and God said to them, 'Be fruitful and multiply, and

---

[3] Oxford English Dictionary, "Gender," at Oxford University Press (6 November 2017), at www.oed.com.

[4] Tabor, "Gender," 671.

fill the earth'" (Gn 1:26-28). Assistant Professor of Theology and Bioethics at Concordia University Irvine, Scott Stiegemeyer, says that God's creation of mankind as male and female "is theologically significant,"[5] and that until the late twentieth century all Christians held to the uncontested doctrine of mankind created as male and female.[6] The Catholic Church subscribes to God's plan expressed in Genesis above, as well, that human beings are created "male and female" in the image of God. The Church recognizes the complementarity of the two genders and their respective masculinity and femininity,[7] testifying to God's willing them "*for* the other."[8] The Church affirms that man and woman together reflect the infinite perfec-

---

[5] Stiegemeyer, 19.

[6] Stiegemeyer, 20.

[7] *Catechism of the Catholic Church*, 2nd ed. (Washington, DC: United States Catholic Conference, 2000), 372.

[8] *CCC*, 371.

tion of God and together cooperate in God's Creation by procreation. [9]

Sara Butler, in her article entitled, "Sex or Gender?," says gender is a principal way we make sense of ourselves as embodied persons such that "no investigation of gender can allow itself to be carried too far off from the body," subsequently quoting John Paul II saying, masculinity and femininity are "two complementary ways of being conscious of the meaning of the body." [10]

THE SOUL DEFINED

The "soul" of the human person, according to the *Catechism of the Catholic Church*, encompasses man's entire being with prominent importance afforded to his "*spiritual principle*" of the intellect and will by which

---

[9] *CCC*, 370.

[10] Sara Butler, "Sex or Gender?," *First Things* 154 (2005), 46.

he conforms "most especially" to God's image.[11] In *The Elements of Philosophy*, William Wallace explains that man is comprised of two essential parts existing in union—a material body and a spiritual soul, and specifies that man's soul differs from the souls of all other living things in that his soul is rational and intellectual.[12] Another renowned Catholic theologian, Ludwig Ott, in *Fundamentals of Catholic Dogma*, says that man's body and soul are connected in such a way that they exist "not merely externally like a vessel and its contents, a ship and its pilot," but as "an intrinsic natural unit."[13]

---

[11] *CCC*, 363, 1711.

[12] William Wallace, *The Elements of Philosophy: A Compendium for Philosophers and* Theologians, 2nd ed. (Eugene, OR: Wipf and Stock Publishers, 2011), 80.

[13] Ludwig Ott, *Fundamentals of Catholic Dogma*, ed. James Canon Bastible, trans. Patrick Lynch (Charoltte, NC: TAN Books, 1974), 97.

Author of *St. Thomas Aquinas*, Ralph McInerny, confers the Doctor of the Church's thoughts that "unlike the substantial forms of all other natural substances, [man's soul] does not exist simply as a result of its composition with matter; rather it has existence and confers existence on the body."[14] This corresponds with Catholic teaching that a human being is precisely human because he/she contains a spiritual soul, which animates the body.[15] Wallace concurs saying that a living body has both "substantial matter and a substantial form," but it is because of the *substantial form of our souls* that "we live, sense, move, and understand."[16] Wallace further articulates the immateriality of man's soul by saying that

---

[14] Ralph McInerny, *St. Thomas Aquinas* (Notre Dame, IN: University of Notre Dame Press, 1982), 47-48.

[15] *CCC*, 364.

[16] Wallace, *Elements of Philosophy*, 61.

the soul comes into being at creation; it is not produced by the generative act of parents; and at the death of the body one's soul lives on as evidenced by one's "unlimited spiritual capacities and desires, and from the necessity of moral sanctions in an afterlife."[17]

GENDER DETERMINANTS

How is one's gender determined? Gender is chiefly determined by the presence of XX or XY chromosomes in one's DNA (producing a female or male, respectively). Some individuals, however, are born with a variety of "intersex" medical conditions involving abnormalities with one's sex organs, hormones, and/or chromosomes.[18] In these cases, how can one be certain about one's gender? Anthropologist, Mary Douglas,

---

[17] Wallace, *Elements of Philosophy*, 82.

[18] Stiegemeyer, 23.

quoted in Scott Stiegemeyer's article, "How Do You Know Whether You Are a Man or a Woman?," says classifying one as either male or female "is a human universal."[19] Stiegemeyer, himself, says that when we initially meet someone new we subconsciously determine gender by assessing one's physical features, clothing, hairstyle, accessories, voice, gestures and the like, feeling discomfort if unable to discern someone's gender.[20] Secondary anatomical sex traits such as the breasts, hips, musculature, Adam's apple, and even one's voice pitch all contribute, in addition, in helping us to discern gender.[21]

As previously mentioned, there are a number of "intersex" conditions that individuals may be born with that cause confusion and uncertainty in determining one's sex. Some individuals are born with 47

---

[19] Stiegemeyer, 21.

[20] Stiegemeyer, 21-22.

[21] Stiegemeyer, 22.

chromosomes, instead of the normal 46, having an additional sex chromosome, and there are other individuals with only 45 sets of chromosomes having a sex chromosome missing.[22] In a *National Catholic Bioethics Quarterly* article, Nicholas Tonti-Filippini says, "These disorders do not result in an intersex condition in which there is discrepancy between internal and external genitalia. Instead, there may be problems with sex hormone levels and overall sexual development."[23]

Other individuals have androgen insensitivity syndrome (AIS) in which one is born with XY chromosomes (indicating male)—however, one's body is unable to assimilate its own testosterone, producing female physical features.[24] Others are born with abnormal genitals that have some semblance of

---

[22] Tonti-Filippini, 87.

[23] Tonti-Filippini, 87.

[24] Stiegemeyer, 25.

both sexes or are indistinct altogether.[25] Stiegemeyer acknowledges, "The discovery of a confusing body raises doubts not just about the particular body in question, but about all bodies."[26] Of significance, he says, is that when an organ or bodily tissue is unable to perform its natural function, it is important to recognize this as an abnormality.[27] He exposes a key point, here, contradicting those who endorse gender as being "non-essential" to human nature. He concludes that *nature itself* is the final arbiter, which admits males and females as distinct and vital for the procreation of the species. He states, "Attitudes toward gender identity these days might not favor the binary, but the human reproductive system does."[28]

---

[25] Stiegemeyer, 25.

[26] Stiegemeyer, 25.

[27] Stiegemeyer, 26.

[28] Stiegemeyer, 26.

Homosexuals are those individuals attracted to members of their own birth sex. Both Mary Jo Anderson and medical doctor Robin Bernhoft, authors of *Male and Female HE MADE THEM: Questions and Answers about Marriage and Same-Sex Unions,* [29] quote Dean Byrd, professor at Brigham Young University and the University of Utah, who says, "Scientific attempts to demonstrate that homosexual attraction is biologically determined have failed," citing "major researchers now prominent in the scientific arena—themselves gay activists— have in fact arrived at such conclusions." [30]

---

[29] Mary Jo Anderson and Robin Bernhoft, *Male and Female HE MADE THEM: Questions and Answers about Marriage and Same-Sex Unions* (San Diego: Catholic Answers, 2005), 78.

[30] Anderson and Bernhoft, *Male and Female*, 78. [Quote from: A. Dean Byrd, "In Their Own Words: Gay Activists Speak About Science, Morality, Philosophy" (www.narth.com/docs/innate.html).]

Byrd cites the work of Dean Hamer, who was trying to link male homosexuality to DNA in his research but was unable. He says, "There is not a single master gene that makes people gay. . . . I don't think we will ever be able to predict who will be gay."[31] If genetics were involved in homosexuality, then identical twins would each experience same-sex attraction, say Anderson and Bernhoft; however, studies reveal that this is not the case with environmental factors providing chief influences on the development of same-sex attraction.[32]

Transgender persons identify with the opposite gender of their birth but may be attracted to those of their opposite birth sex *or* to those of their natural birth sex (in which case they are also homosexual). Those that are transsexual desire and work to tran-

---

[31] Anderson and Bernhoft, 79. [Quote from: Byrd, "In Their Own Words."]

[32] Anderson and Bernhoft, 79.

sition themselves to their opposite birth sex via hormones and/or surgery.[33] Gender dysphoria (formerly called Gender Identity Disorder) is another condition in which an individual has a "rare and puzzling state of extreme and, at times, debilitating discomfort with one's natal sex."[34] In this condition, the individual has the sense that their natural born gender is not in correspondence with their sense of self. Stiegemeyer says this title change, in the latest edition of the Diagnostic and Statistical Manual of Mental Disorders (DSM-5) from "disorder" to "dysphoria," shifts the emphasis "from being a disorder in the person's identity to being an unwanted emotional state," saying the transgender community wishes "to divorce their concerns from the stigma of mental illness."[35] Stiegemeyer says it is of interest to

---

[33] Stiegemeyer, 33.

[34] Stiegemeyer, 20.

[35] Stiegemeyer, 30.

note that 73% of children who experience gender dysphoria in childhood report they no longer suffer with it in adulthood, making it seem a possibility that some remainder of cases may be aided by psychotherapy and/or medication in an attempt to successfully realign one's feelings of identify with one's gender of birth. [36]

There are also individuals that suffer from Body Dysmorphic Disorder (BDD). This is a disorder in which an individual strongly believes that his/her body is "ugly or incorrect in some manner" and wishes to change it—akin to those who suffer with eating disorders or Body Integrity Identity Disorder (BIID), which is having a persistent desire to amputate otherwise healthy limbs to match an "idealized image" of oneself. [37]

Stiegemeyer expresses two main hypotheses of how one's gender identity, prefer-

---

[36] Stiegemeyer, 32.

[37] Stiegemeyer, 34-35.

ence, and behavior originate. He first cites a psychological hypothesis which holds that males and females are essentially different in their makeup—including within their brains that develop differently in utero—resulting in one's having a subjective internal sense of being male or female according to one's nature.[38] The second hypothesis is a sociological hypothesis that males and females are not psychologically different at birth, nor do they possess any meaningful brain differences; there are only human beings, with society ascribing male and female categories.[39]

One may wonder if sex reassignment surgery aids those who undergo such treatment for their disorders. Stiegemeyer quotes Paul McHugh, head of the psychiatry department at John Hopkins Hospital, who stopped these surgeries from continuing at

---

[38] Stiegemeyer, 27.

[39] Stiegemeyer, 27.

his hospital in 1979 because he witnessed two flawed assumptions of current treatments: 1) that humans were neutral to sexual identity at birth, and 2) that postnatal cultural influences were most responsible for sexual identity.[40]

McHugh, in his article, "Surgical Sex," says he decided to (1) study men who underwent sex change operations to become women to see if their psychological problems resolved, post-surgery, in feeling that their bodies were now aligned with their true inner selves; and (2) to study males who had undergone operations to become females as infants due to ambiguous genitalia, and who were subsequently raised as girls, to see how they fared into adulthood.[41] Of the men who chose as adults to undergo transitional surgery, McHugh says that although

---

[40] Stiegemeyer, 30.

[41] Paul McHugh, "Surgical Sex," *First Things* 147 (2004), 34.

many tell him the surgery made them content, he is not persuaded because they had no change in terms of resolving previous problems and emotional difficulties with which they struggled prior to surgery.[42] Moreover, says McHugh, these surgical subjects appear "caricatures of women"— wearing high heels, makeup, clothing, and the like—but whose "large hands, prominent Adam's apples, and thick facial features" are incongruent with their proclaimed sex— things, he says, that will only contrast more as they age.[43] Of more remarkable note, he says, is the fact that these men-turned- "women" report being sexually attracted to women, not men.[44]

Sixteen genetic male infants from Johns Hopkins Hospital were also studied who had been born with cloacal exstrophy, a condi-

---

[42] McHugh, 35.

[43] McHugh, 34.

[44] McHugh, 34.

tion in which the penis fails to form and one's bladder and urinary tract are not separated from the gastrointestinal tract.[45] Pediatric endocrinologists and psychologists, McHugh says, persuaded the parents of the infants to go through with sex change operations on their sons informing them that their children's sexual identity "would simply conform to environmental conditioning."[46] Fourteen of the males with this condition underwent the selective surgery and were raised as girls, while two of the sixteen's children's parents chose not to elect the surgery for their sons and raised them as boys. Upon follow-up, eight males who had undergone surgery to become females later declared themselves male; five continued living as females; one lived with an unclear sexual identity; and the two males who had not un-

---

[45] McHugh, 36.

[46] McHugh, 35.

dergone surgery and were raised as males, remained male.[47]

All sixteen of the genetic males reported male interests and tendencies such as "vigorous play, sexual arousal by females, and physical aggressiveness" along with enjoyment of such things as "hunting, ice hockey, karate, and bobsledding."[48] Stiegemeyer says it is true that there is overlap in the gender expression human beings demonstrate in terms of the typical male/female traits they may possess—for example, some men display more nurturing female traits and some women more assertive male-type traits. That being said, Stiegemeyer says, "it is a critical overstatement to say that one's body has *nothing* to do with one's gender."[49] The resident psychiatrist at John Hopkins who undertook the study of these males-

---

[47] McHugh, 36-37.

[48] McHugh, 37.

[49] Stiegemeyer, 27.

transformed-into-"females" in infancy was William G. Reiner. McHugh says:

> Reiner, however, discovered that such re-engineered males were almost never comfortable as females once they became aware of themselves and the world. From the start of their active play life, they behaved spontaneously like boys and were obviously different from their sisters and other girls, enjoying rough-and-tumble games but not dolls and "playing house." Later on, most of those individuals who learned that they were actually genetic males wished to reconstitute their lives as males (some even asked for surgical reconstruction and male hormone replacement)—and all this despite the earnest efforts by their parents to treat them as girls. [50]

---

[50] McHugh, 36.

"With these facts in hand," says McHugh, "I concluded that Hopkins was fundamentally cooperating with a mental illness,"[51] with his department concluding, as well, that "human sexual identity is mostly built into our constitution by the genes we inherit and the embryogenesis we undergo."[52] Many other hospitals followed suit and stopped these surgeries as well. He says, "there is a deep prejudice in favor of the idea that nature is totally malleable;" however, "without any fixed position on what is given in human nature, any manipulation of it can be defended as legitimate."[53]

Leon Suprenant, Jr., and Philip Gray, authors of *Faith Facts: Answers to Catholic Questions*, say that having a disordered sexual attraction towards someone of the same sex (as in homosexuality) does not make the

---

[51] McHugh, 35.

[52] McHugh, 37.

[53] McHugh, 37-38.

disordered inclination in and of itself sinful. It is homosexual *acts* that are always objectively and intrinsically disordered and "gravely contrary to chastity" as states the *Catechism* in paragraph 2396.[54] Anderson and Bernhoft expand that "objectively," homosexuality "is a disorder" because "logically, homosexual acts are not ordered to the function that corresponds to their biological structure. Thus they are dis-ordered, against order, against nature."[55]

Mutilation of any healthy organs and tissues, performed during sex change operations, is also morally illicit, says John Paul II, repeating in *Redemptor Hominis* a passage from the Second Vatican Council, which states:

---

[54] Leon J. Suprenant, Jr. and Philip C.L. Gray, *Faith Facts: Answers to Catholic Questions*, vol.1 (Steubenville, OH: Emmaus Road Publishing, 1999), 120.

[55] Anderson and Bernhoft, 75.

> Whatever is opposed to life itself, such as any type of murder, genocide, abortion, euthanasia, or willful self-destruction, whatever violates the integrity of the human person, such as mutilation . . . whatever insults human dignity . . . are infamies indeed. They poison human society, and they do more harm to those who practice them than to those who suffer from the injury. Moreover, they are a supreme dishonour [*sic*] to the Creator.[56]

Sterilization is also always wrong, says the Church, "even when it is motivated by a subjectively right intention of curing or preventing a physical or psychological ill-effect

---

[56] John Paul II, Encyclical on the Gospel of Life, *Evangelium Vitae* (25 March 1995), §3 (Boston: Pauline Books & Media, 1995), 14. (John Paul II's quote is taken from the Pastoral Constitution on the Church in the Modern World *Gaudium et Spes*, 27.)

that is foreseen or feared" in that it renders "the generative faculty incapable of procreation."[57] The reason for this is that "sterility induced . . . does not contribute to the person's integral good . . . rather, it does damage to a person's ethical good, which is the highest since it deprives subsequent freely chosen sexual acts of an essential element."[58] Pope John Paul goes on to say that those in the medical profession, whose duty it is to uphold and aid human life, and who subsequently engage in acts such as mutilation and sterilization of the human person, contradict their profession and degrade their own dignity.[59]

Tonti-Filippini says that if gender dysphoria was shown to have a biological cause

---

[57] Heinrich Denzinger, *Compendium of Creeds, Definitions, and Declarations on Matters of Faith and Morals*, ed. Peter Hünermann (San Francisco: Ignatius Press, 2012), 1007.

[58] Denzinger, *Compendium*, 1008.

[59] *Evangelium Vitae*, §4.

the Catholic Church would almost certainly still not endorse sex reassignment surgery because this treatment involves destroying healthy biology instead of restoring normal function, and because of its implications for human sexuality in light of the procreative meaning attached to the gift of the generative act.[60] This view is backed up by biological facts, states Tonti-Filippini, because:

(1) the body seeks to revert to the phenotype associated with the genotype if hormonal treatment is stopped; (2) the treatment provides a change that is more cosmetic than real; and (3) evidence of the success of the treatment for the psychological disorder is equivocal . . . What happens, in fact, is the destruction of normal healthy organs; the person's gender is left essentially as the gender at birth, requiring continual hormonal in-

---

[60] Tonti-Filippini, 94.

terventions to suppress the body's natural tendency to revert to gender type.[61]

"It is essential to understand," says Stiegemeyer, "that psychological conditions are corporeal afflictions to the extent that our thoughts, will, desires, and memories are grounded in the material substance of the brain."[62]

THE BRAIN DIFFERENCE

Differences exist between the male and female brains, as well. "Differences are not deficiencies," declare Susan Case and Angela Oetama-Paul, authors of an article entitled, "Brain Biology and Gendered Discourse," saying that men and women possess differences in "brain structure, function, and chemistry" producing "gendered communi-

---

[61] Tonti-Filippini, 94.

[62] Stiegemeyer, 47.

cation styles influenced by biology."[63] Women, say Case and Oetama-Paul, possess a normative feminine "affiliative style" by which they foster relationships using communication to show support, affirmation, and understanding, and in positions of authority they are generally more polite than men.[64] Men, on the other hand, possess a normative masculine "assertive style," using talk as a means of control to demonstrate autonomy and status, they are also competitive, and use speech to influence others to action.[65]

The various brain structures of men and women differ. The ventral frontal cortex, responsible for social cognition, relational judgment, and decision-making, is larger in

---

[63] Susan S. Case and Angela J. Oetama-Paul, "Brain Biology and Gendered Discourse," *Applied Psychology: An International Review* 64, no. 2 (2015), 338, 342.

[64] Case and Oetama-Paul, 344.

[65] Case and Oetama-Paul, 344-345.

women causing them to have greater interpersonal awareness, interpretation of non-
verbal cues, and ability to perceive anger
than men.[66] Patterns of blood flow also differ in the brains of males and females. Blood
flow in men flows through "spatial-
mechanical centers in the right hemisphere,"
an area of "kinesthetic intelligence and ab-
straction," and blood flow in women's brains
runs through "emotive centers" connecting
"memories, emotions, sensory and context
cues (Cosgrove et al., 2007)."[67] The brain
blood flow in women's mid brain cingulate
gyrus coordinates sensory input concerning
emotions, enabling women's attention to
voice tone, gestures and facial expressions,
compared with men's cingulate gyrus blood
flow facilitating the male ability to hone in
and directly focus on tasks and outcomes.[68]

---

[66] Case and Oetama-Paul, 348.

[67] Case and Oetama-Paul, 348.

[68] Case and Oetama-Paul, 348.

Blood flow within the female brain is twenty percent greater between hemispheres than blood flow in the male brain, supporting a theory that women use both hemispheres at the same time to process information, listen, and talk, in contrast with men's brains that seemingly divide tasks between hemispheres, giving them a greater ability for intense focus.[69] These lateralization theories are still just theories, with some scientists very confident that female brains are the more bilaterally organized, and men's more lateralized, while other scientists require more empirical evidence to be convinced.[70] Specialization of hemispheres, nevertheless, begins prior to birth, bilaterally, as early as four weeks of age.[71]

The corpus callosum, consisting of neural fibers connecting the right and left hemi-

---

[69] Case and Oetama-Paul, 348-349.

[70] Case and Oetama-Paul, 349.

[71] Case and Oetama-Paul, 351.

spheres of the brain, may also constitute a point of difference between the sexes with women having a larger, more bulbous corpus callosum—affording them greater information exchange, in contrast to men who have a more elongated corpus callosum. Inconsistencies exist, however, concerning corpus callosum size due to the aging process in both male and female brains.[72]

Interesting findings continue concerning the gray and white matter found within different sections of male and female brains. Gray matter contains the brain's chief information-processing center; white matter houses the brain's information-processing networks.[73] Women have more gray matter than white; men more white matter than gray; women possess more white and gray matter in their frontal lobes; men have no gray in their frontal lobes, but more gray in

---

[72] Case and Oetama-Paul, 349.

[73] Case and Oetama-Paul, 350.

their parietal lobes.[74] The gray matter in men processes information within one hemisphere, helping them focus on tasks without being distracted and burdened by particulars, while gray matter in women disseminates information they are able to process all at once all the while memories and emotions are simultaneously being taken into account.[75] Women possess a larger hippocampus housing the brain's memory center than men and have more neural pathways enabling them to retrieve "interactive details from the past" and possess "greater understanding of situational subtleties" than men.[76] Men's smaller hippocampus is linked to less emotional sharing and reduced interactive details, providing men the ability to rapidly move forward and make decisions.[77]

---

[74] Case and Oetama-Paul, 350.

[75] Case and Oetama-Paul, 350.

[76] Case and Oetama-Paul, 350.

[77] Case and Oetama-Paul, 351.

Emotional processing within the brains of men and women differs, too. The female amygdala is "more strongly activated in processing emotion than men's," with men having a more "doing brain" searching for "practical solutions, ignoring much information that women notice (Eliot, 2009)."[78] Women also have more densely packed nerve cells than men in their occipital and parietal lobes allowing them to hear better and take action.[79] Women "nod, establish eye contact, smile, and ask more questions than men to understand," as opposed to men who "listen for facts to get straight to the point, with little eye contact," and who interrupt more with a quick offer of a solution upon hearing about a problem.[80]

Differences in language specialization between the brains of the sexes are subtle;

---

[78] Case and Oetama-Paul, 355-356.

[79] Case and Oetama-Paul, 351.

[80] Case and Oetama-Paul, 351.

however, women have verbal abilities and emotional centers that exist in both hemispheres of their brains, while men primarily use their left hemisphere for language and the right for emotions.[81] Attention differences are also appreciated amongst the sexes. A 2000 study conducted with 102 one-day old infants revealed that when these newborns saw a human face or a colorful mobile with hanging ball attached, girl babies "preferred faces, especially eyes," while boy babies preferred "inanimate objects, demonstrating, in part, differences of biological origin" (Connellan, Baron-Cohen, Wheelwright, Batki, & Ahluwalia, 2000).[82]

Hormonal influences affect brain chemistry in each gender, as well, with hormones playing a varying role in males and females with respect to age. In utero, hormonal levels of testosterone are ten times higher in

---

[81] Case and Oetama-Paul, 352.

[82] Case and Oetama-Paul, 353.

boys than in girls.[83] The testosterone link "to aggression," say Case and Oetama-Paul, "is one of the largest, most reliable, and likely innate male/female differences (Eliot, 2009)."[84] After winning a competition, men's testosterone levels are higher than women's which drops or remains flat.[85] Higher testosterone levels in men may be the reason men are more competitive, direct, less nurturing, etc., in the workplace than women, and why in their socialization they are "devoted to displaying power and protecting competitive systems of relationships."[86] Women possess more estrogen, progesterone, and oxytocin, influencing lower aggression, more sociability, social memory, trust, and relationship building.[87]

---

[83] Case and Oetama-Paul, 358.

[84] Case and Oetama-Paul, 358.

[85] Case and Oetama-Paul, 358.

[86] Case and Oetama-Paul, 359.

[87] Case and Oetama-Paul, 359.

In a 2007 study in which men were given small doses of female hormones, their ability to read emotions increased (Domes, Heinrichs, Michel, Berger & Herpetz, 2007).[88] As testosterone levels decline for men after approximately age fifty, "men's leadership and discourse styles shift to ones including more expressiveness and emotional attention to others;" and as hormone levels decline with age in both of the sexes, their behavior becomes more similar.[89]

Concluding their brain/gender discourse, Case and Oetama-Paul express, "The question is not, 'are there brain differences?'" between the sexes, but rather, "how are we going to respond to brain differences?", citing the value of "linking biology to normatively masculine and normatively feminine" gendered styles in our under-

---

[88] Case and Oetama-Paul, 359.

[89] Case and Oetama-Paul, 357-358.

standing of men and women in the workplace and in society.[90]

Laura L. Garcia, contributor to *Women,
Sex & the Church: A Case for Catholic Teaching*, concurs:

> Current research in biology and in the
> social sciences overwhelmingly supports
> the claim that there are deep-seated bio-
> logical and chemical-based differences
> between girls and boys, women and
> men. . . . scientific evidence from fields
> as diverse as anthropology and neurolo-
> gy is also producing a steady stream of
> data in support of received wisdom on
> this subject . . . . differences between
> males and females are inscribed in our
> very brains.[91]

---

[90] Case and Oetama-Paul, 365, 370.

[91] Laura L. Garcia, "Authentic Freedom and
Equality in Difference," in *Women, Sex & the
Church: A Case for Catholic Teaching*, ed. Erika

Garcia acknowledges Steven Rhoads, professor of government and foreign affairs at the University of Virginia, who in an exhaustive sex difference literature review concludes, says Garcia, that "empirical evidence for deep-seated and important differences between males and females is overwhelming."[92] Garcia points to John Paul II, who in his approach celebrates the differences between men and women, remarking that "he acknowledges, even glories in, the differences between the sexes" attesting to their equal dignity and need of one another, praising differences "that enrich each partner in the relationship, so that the resulting combination is greater than the sum of its parts."[93]

Bachiochi (Boston: Pauline Books & Media, 2010), 22, 23.

[92] Garcia, 23.

[93] Garcia, 16.

Thomas Aquinas agrees, saying, "Just as, considering the nature of the individual, a different quantity is due to different men, so also, considering the nature of the individual, a different sex is due to different men. Moreover, this same diversity is becoming to the perfection of the species, the different degrees whereof are filled by this very difference of sex and quantity."[94] He also says, with regard to the true nature of humanity, "Accordingly a thing is said to belong to the truth of human nature, because it belongs properly to the being of human nature, and this is what shares the form of human nature, just as true gold is what has the true form of gold whence gold derives its proper

---

[94] Thomas Aquinas, *Summa theologiae*, Supplement, q. 81, a. 3, in *Summa theologica*, trans. Fathers of the English Dominican Province (London: Burns Oates & Washbourne, 1921), Verbum: Logos Bible Software.

being."[95] In other words, the truths about human nature are fixed, as are truths to determine if an element is gold. The reason for the differences between the sexes is that they complete what is lacking in the other; they perfect one another by their very difference and diversity when they come together in relationship.

In the next chapter the connection between the human soul and body will be more deeply examined, solidifying the inseparable link that exists between the two in the nature of the human person.

---

[95] *ST*, Supplement, q. 80, a. 4, resp., trans. English Dominican Province, Verbum: Logos Bible Software.

CHAPTER 2
THE BODY/SOUL COMPOSITE

CATHOLIC TEACHING REGARDING THE BODY/SOUL COMPOSITE

The union of man's body and soul is so profound, says the Church, that the soul, as mentioned in the last chapter, is considered both the form and animator of the body.[1] William Wallace says man's body exists because the soul exists and that this distinct ontological relationship demonstrates that the body is an integral part of man's nature.[2] Even though the soul is immaterial, he says, it nevertheless depends on the body for its vegetative and sensitive powers of nutrition, growth, reproduction, sight, hearing, touch, taste, and memory such that "man's soul is

---

[1] *CCC*, 364-365.

[2] Wallace, *Elements of Philosophy*, 81.

incomplete in species when not joined to his body."[3] Early Fathers of the Church, such as Justin Martyr, Tatian, and Athenagoras, were the first to explain this body/soul composition of man, with Irenaeus and Tertullian in the second and third centuries clarifying the soul's spiritual property.[4] Fathers Augustine, Origen, Gregory Nazianzen, and Hilary proclaim man's soul does not come into existence before the body,[5] and Irenaeus, Tertullian, and Aphraates attest to the fact that when God fashions man He does so immediately.[6]

Ludwig Ott illustrates that these two essential parts—body and soul— "will again be resolved into two parts"[7] at the resurrection

---

[3] Wallace, 81-82.

[4] John R. Willis (ed), *The Teachings of the Church Fathers* (San Francisco: Ignatius Press, 2002), 202.

[5] Willis (ed), 202.

[6] Willis (ed), 202.

[7] Ott, *Fundamentals*, 97.

of the body. McInerny, relaying the thoughts of Aquinas, says that Christians believe in a general resurrection of the body when one's body will be reunited with one's soul.[8] He says that the separation of soul and body at death cannot be known apart from Christ's revelation.[9] Joel Green in *Body, Soul, and Human Life: The Nature of Humanity in the Bible* points out that this is in contrast with the Jewish understanding of the body and soul at death which did not foresee "the liberation of the immortal soul from the mortal body."[10]

Our weak bodies help our souls to love God, announces Bernard of Clairvaux, and it is because of this aid to our soul, afforded by

---

[8] McInerny, *St. Thomas Aquinas*, 49.

[9] McInerny, 49.

[10] Joel B. Green, *Body, Soul, and Human Life: The Nature of Humanity in the Bible*. Studies in Theological Interpretation, eds. Craig G. Bartholomew and Christopher R. Seitz (Grand Rapids, MI: Baker Academic, 2008), 151.

the body, that one's soul wishes to be reunited after death with one's glorified body:[11]

> Truly, the soul does not want to be perfected without that which it feels has served it well in every condition . . . . It is not in dispute that they [souls] want their bodies back; if they thus desire and hope for them, it is clear that they have not wholly turned from themselves, for it is evident that they are still clinging to something which is their own, even if their desires return to it only a very little. Until death is swallowed up in victory (1 Cor 15:54), and the everlasting light invades the farthest bounds of night and shines everywhere—so that heavenly glory gleams even in bodies—these souls cannot wholly remove themselves and

---

[11] Bernard of Clairvaux, *Bernard of Clairvaux: Selected Works*, ed. John Farina, trans. G. R. Evans (New York: Paulist Press, 1987), 197.

transport themselves to God. They are still too much bound to their bodies, if not in life and feeling, certainly in natural affection. They do not wish to be complete without them, and indeed they cannot.[12]

In 1 Corinthians, Paul acknowledges Christ as the first example of bodily resurrection for his believers, his Church, avowing, "Christ has been raised from the dead, the first fruits of those who have died" (1 Cor 15:20). Paul admits that our bodies will be changed at the resurrection, but James Ware, in an article entitled "Paul's Understanding of the Resurrection in 1 Corinthians 15:36-54,"[13] says that the "'change' Paul envisions for the risen body . . . involves a

---

[12] Bernard of Clairvaux, 197.

[13] James Ware, "Paul's Understanding of the Resurrection in 1 Corinthians 15:36-54," *Journal of Biblical Literature* 133, no. 4 (2014), 835.

change in its qualities rather than a destruction of its substance," saying that the language Paul uses refers to the "fleshly body"
given new life by the power of the Holy Spirit (1 Cor 15:52). Ware likens this to the Jewish understanding of a body resurrected after death by the power of God gleaned from
Scripture in such passages as Is 26:11-19, Dn
12:2-3, among others.[14] The Evangelist John,
author of the biblical books of John, also up-
holds, "We are God's children now;
what we will be has not yet been revealed.
What we do know is this: when he is revealed, we will be like him, for we will see
him as he is (1 Jn 3:2)."

AQUINAS'S TEACHING ON THE
BODY/SOUL COMPOSITE

Aquinas confirms that since the union of
man's body and soul is natural, the perfec-

---

[14] Ware, 835.

tion of the soul cannot be complete until it is again reunited with the body. Unless and until this occurs, the soul "cannot have the ultimate perfection of beatitude."[15] Origen, early father and theologian of the Church, sees the resurrection of our actual bodies as logically necessary, moreover, because ultimately "one eternal thing [the soul] cannot be contrary to another eternal thing [the body]," and that "when the last enemy, the death *of the soul* will be destroyed," our bodies will rise, and the Enemy will then truly and exceedingly be destroyed.[16]

Regarding the body/soul composite, Aquinas affirms, "all the members that are

---

[15] Thomas Aquinas, *Quaestiones Disputatae de Potentia Dei: On the Power of God*, q. 5, a. 10, at Dominican House of Studies Priory of the Immaculate Conception, www.dhspriory.org.

[16] Christoph Heilig, "Resurrection and the Eoundation [*sic*] of Christian Behaviour: Paul and Origen in Dialogue," *Colloquium* 46, no. 2 (2014), 196.

now in man's body must needs be restored at the resurrection."[17] To emphasize the integrity of body and soul in the resurrection, Aquinas declares that even our *blood* will rise again.[18] Because our resurrection will be conformed to Christ's, and *his* blood rose again—for if it did not his blood would not now be able to be changed into the Sacrament of the altar—then it positions that our blood "will rise again in us also, in like manner the other humours."[19] Ott corresponds, "The integrity of the body after its resurrection also demands the organs of vegetative and sensitive life, including the differences between the sexes."[20] He explains that at the resurrection our bodies will be free from all

---

[17] *ST*, Supplement, q. 80, a. 1, resp., trans. English Dominican Province, Verbum: Logos Bible Software.

[18] *ST*, Supplement, q. 80, a. 3, sc.

[19] *ST*, Supplement, q. 80, a. 3, sc.

[20] Ott, *Fundamentals*, 491.

maladies and defects and rise complete.[21] Aquinas asserts this as well, saying:

> If anything belonging to the truth of human nature in a man be taken from his body, this will not be the perfect body of a man. Now all imperfection of a man will be removed at the resurrection. . . . therefore whatever belonged to the truth of human nature in a man will rise again in him.[22]

It is certain then that at the resurrection all abnormalities in man—including those involving one's sex chromosomes, hormones, and/or organs, will be perfected in him. Stiegemeyer affirms, "We remember that Christ's love for the heavily burdened is

---

[21] Ott, 491.

[22] *ST*, Supplement, q. 80, a. 4, sc.

paramount and that the results of the fall will be undone on the Last Day." [23]

Responding to those in his day who thought that only men would rise in the resurrection, Aquinas explains, "At the resurrection God will restore man to what He made him at the creation. Now He made woman from the man's rib (Gen 2:22). Therefore He will also restore the female sex at the resurrection." [24] Accordingly, says Aquinas, "each one will rise again of that quantity which would have been his at the end of his growth if nature had not erred or failed: and the Divine power will subtract or supply what was excessive or lacking in man." [25] John Paul declares that historical man differs from eschatological man who will have complete freedom from the opposition between body and soul. The spiritual-

---

[23] Stiegemeyer, 44.

[24] *ST*, Supplement, q. 81, a. 3, sc.

[25] *ST*, Supplement, q. 81, a. 2, resp.

ization of man that occurs post resurrection will *"fully permeate the body and the powers of the spirit will permeate the energies of the body"*[26] such that body and soul will exist in perfect harmony.

JOHN PAUL II'S TEACHING ON THE BODY/SOUL COMPOSITE

In *Man and Woman He Created Them: A Theology of the Body*, John Paul II points to the synoptic gospels of Matthew, Mark, and Luke which all observe human beings regaining their perfected bodies in the resurrection as proper images of God including "their masculinity and femininity."[27] Donald

---

[26] Pope John Paul II, General Audience (9 December 1981), in *Man and Woman He Created Them: A Theology of the Body*, trans. Michael Waldstein (Boston: Pauline Books & Media, 2006), 67:1, p. 391.

[27] John Paul II, General Audience (2 December 1981), trans. Waldstein 66:1, p. 387.

H. Calloway, editor of *The Virgin Mary and Theology of the Body*, says that John Paul's "theological anthropology is the fact that . . . every human body, is a gendered body," which implies that our gender is more than just temporal, but actually eternal.[28] John Paul II says that the reason for our bodies, and specifically for being a male or female body, has everything to do with marriage, procreation, fatherhood and motherhood."[29] The reason God commands man and woman to "be fruitful and multiply," says Calloway, is training for our understanding of the image of God in the Trinity.[30] Through the exchange of love between a man and woman in marriage, a third—a child—results, akin, in a way, to the love between the Father and

---

[28] Donald H. Calloway (ed), *The Virgin Mary and Theology of the Body* (Stockbridge, MA: Marian Press, 2005), 51.

[29] John Paul II, General Audience (13 January 1982), trans. Waldstein, 69:4, p. 399.

[30] Calloway (ed), 48-49.

the Son, who, together, Spirate the Holy Spirit.[31]

Pablo Gadenz, contributor to *Catholic for a Reason: Scripture and the Mystery of the Family of God*, expresses that God provides our descent from Adam and Eve, our first parents, to join humanity into "one united family."[32] Additionally, Gadenz quotes John Paul II that man and woman exist in familial relationship and communion with one another in love to image our relationship with God and to mirror "the divine communion"[33] of the Trinity.

Commenting on Luke's gospel, which proclaims that those that rise from the dead "neither marry nor are given in marriage"

---

[31] Calloway (ed), 49.

[32] Pablo Gadenz, "The Church as the Family of God," in *Catholic for a Reason: Scripture and the Mystery of the Family of God*, ed. Scott Hahn and Leon J. Suprenant, Jr. (Steubenville, OH: Emmaus Road Publishing, 1998), 82.

[33] Gadenz, 81-82.

(Lk 20:35), John Paul II says that this passage contains a *key* meaning for the theology of the body.[34] Marriage is established by God in Gn 2:24 when God commands man to unite with his wife and to become "one flesh." This union, says John Paul II, is significant for man's earthly life; however, in the resurrection marriage and procreation are not part of man's eschatological future because in the afterlife "they lose . . . their *raison* d'être [purpose]."[35] He enlightens that although man and woman will retain their masculinity and femininity in their eschatological future, "*the meaning of being male or female in the body* will be *constituted and understood differently*" than from man's beginning.[36] The life to come which Luke speaks about, says John Paul II, constitutes

---

[34] John Paul II, General Audience (2 December 1981), trans. Waldstein, 66:1, p. 387.

[35] John Paul II, 66:2, p. 387.

[36] John Paul II, 66:4, p. 388.

"the quantitative closure of that circle of beings created in the image and likeness of God in order that, multiplying through the conjugal 'unity of the body' of men and women, they would subdue the earth to themselves."[37]

John Paul II further says that man does not transform into a purely angelic spirit in the life to come, as is the nature of angels, but retains *his own nature*, which necessitates his "psychosomatic nature," saying, "If it were otherwise, it would be meaningless to speak about the resurrection."[38] Aquinas agrees, saying that man's body does not change into a spirit at the resurrection because "there is no community of matter between them" and if "one's body were changed into a spirit, one would not rise

---

[37] John Paul II, 66:2 p. 387-388.

[38] John Paul II, 66:5 p. 389.

again a man, for a man naturally consists of a soul and body."[39]

John Paul II references Psalm 8:5 which says, "You have made him [man] little less than the angels," and he says, "one must suppose" man's likeness to the angels must indeed "be greater" in the resurrection because of the spiritualization that occurs to man when his body comes into complete submission to his soul.[40] He reiterates, as well, what Aquinas, Origen, and Ott describe that in the resurrection man will be in perfect soul-body harmony, thus he will no longer experience the spiritual warfare of the body against the soul.[41]

John Paul II regards Aquinas's recognition that the body is not momentarily linked

---

[39] *ST*, Supplement, q. 83, a. 1, resp., trans. English Dominican Province, Verbum: Logos Bible Software.

[40] John Paul II, 66:5 p. 389.

[41] John Paul II, 67:1, p. 391.

with the soul but, rather, forms a complete unity with the soul such that:

> The truth about the resurrection clearly affirms that man's eschatological perfection and happiness cannot be understood as a state of the soul alone, separated ... from the body, but must be understood as *the definitively and perfectly 'integrated' state of man* brought about by such a union of the soul with the body that it definitively qualifies and assures this perfect integrity.[42]

Upon the resurrection of man's body, says John Paul II, the Trinitarian God will make man's individual personhood "emerge in an incomparably greater and fuller measure" to exist in everlasting communion with Him and the saints of heaven.[43] Man will

---

[42] John Paul II, 66:6, p. 390.

[43] John Paul II, 67:3, p. 392-393.

rediscover himself in a *"new, perfect inter-subjectivity of all"* involving profound knowledge and self-realization pertaining to the true "'spousal' meaning of the body" culminating in a "perfect realization of the 'trinitarian order' in the created world of persons."[44]

---

[44] John Paul II, 67:4, p. 395-396.

CHAPTER 3
THE GLORIFIED BODY

CHRIST'S RESURRECTED BODY

One needs only look at the Scriptures to admit of Jesus' resurrection from the dead and his appearances to many—including his apostles, disciples, Mary Magdalene, and others between his resurrection and ascension into Heaven—often appearing to many individuals at the same time. Peter Kreeft and Ronald Tacelli, authors of *Handbook of Catholic Apologetics: Reasoned Answers to Questions of Faith*, say that Christ's resurrection is not a case of reincarnation, it is not a case of witnesses seeing a ghost, it is not a vision, it is not legend, nor is it a case of resuscitation.[1] "Unlike myths," they say, Jesus'

---

[1] Peter J. Kreeft and Ronald K. Tacelli, *Handbook of Catholic Apologetics: Reasoned An-*

resurrection "is pinned down to a real, specific, concrete time and place in history and certified by eyewitnesses."[2]

Scriptures Mk 16:9; Mk 16:12; Lk 24:13-43; Jn 20:19-28; Jn 21:1; and Jn 21:12-14 all exhibit Jesus' return after his resurrection. In Luke 24, Jesus specifically walks, talks, and "breaks bread" with the disciples he meets on the road to Emmaus. In John 20, Jesus tells Thomas to put his hand into his side, his finger into his hands, and to *believe*; and later in Luke 24:41-43 Jesus *physically* eats a piece of broiled fish in the presence of his disciples. In all these accounts, Jesus is recognized in his human male body. In reiterating the words of Paul in 1 Cor 15:20 from the last chapter, "Christ has been raised from the dead, the first fruits of those who have died," we are reminded that Christ is

---

swers to Questions of Faith (San Francisco: Ignatius Press, 2009), 189-191.

[2] Kreeft and Tacelli, 191.

the first to rise among us after his atoning death for our sins is accomplished, and his bodily resurrection is the prime example of what our own bodily resurrection will look like. Paul writes, "If the Spirit of him who raised Jesus from the dead dwells in you, he who raised Christ from the dead will give life to your mortal bodies also through his Spirit that dwells in you (Rom 8:11)." John Paul II recants, "Thus, in Christ 'all will rise again with the bodies which they now bear' (Fourth Lateran Council, DS 801), but this body of ours will be changed into a glorious body (cf. Phil 3:21), into a 'spiritual body' (1 Cor 15:44)." [3] Harkening back to John's words, "We will be like him, for we will see him as he is (1 Jn 3:2)," recalls those who *do* physically see Jesus between his resurrection

---

[3] Pope John Paul II, General Audience on Our Bodies Will Share in the Resurrection (4 November 1998), *L'Osservatore Romano* 1566 (1998), 11.

and ascension "*as he is.*" Although his body appears somewhat different, as it can walk through walls—demonstrated in John 20:19—he is still very much recognizable in his discernable male body with his familiar features.

THE IMPLICATIONS OF CHRIST'S RESURRECTION FOR OUR OWN RESURRECTED BODIES

Peter Kreeft, author of *Everything You Ever Wanted to Know about Heaven . . . but Never Dreamed of Asking*, makes an important observation regarding bible passages John 20:14-16, where Mary Magdalene does not recognize Jesus at first until he says to her, "'Mary!;'" Luke 24:15-31, when the disciples do not recognize Jesus in Emmaus until he takes bread, blesses it, breaks it, and gives it to them; and passage John 21:1-7, when from the shore Jesus tells his disciples to cast their nets overboard to catch some fish. Kreeft points out that it is not until an *action* or *word* from Christ takes place that these individuals are able to recognize him, revealing that our present way of recognizing someone—via the body—seems to be reversed in the life to come—recognizing body through character.[4] Kreeft says this is indicative of the new body/soul relationship, not subject to The Fall, that we will experience in the afterlife because as, "the perfected soul is perfectly subject to God, the perfected body can be perfectly subject to the soul, for the soul's authority over the body is a delegated and dependent authority."[5] John Paul II also says this inability of those to initially recognize Christ in his resurrected body reveals, "a certain element of fear in his presence. He is loved, he is sought, but when

---

[4] Peter Kreeft, *Everything You Ever Wanted to Know about Heaven . . . but Never Dreamed of Asking* (San Francisco: Ignatius Press, 1990), 99.

[5] Kreeft, 99.

found, there is a certain hesitation."[6] He infers a psychological process taking place in those that meet Christ between his resurrection and ascension because they see Jesus the same as he always was, yet they also perceive a *difference* in him such that they are filled with fear, love, and reverence.[7]

In Luke 24:39, Jesus tells his disciples, "'Look at my hands and my feet; see that it is I myself. Touch me and see; for a ghost does not have flesh and bones as you see that I have.' And when he had said this, he showed them his hands and his feet." Jesus retains his very bones in his resurrected body. Our resurrected body will mimic Christ's, maintaining our gender, too, as did Christ's. Says Aquinas, both sexes are required "for the

---

[6] Pope John Paul II, General Audience on Characteristics of the Apparitions of the Risen Christ (22 February 1989), *L'Osservatore Romano* 1078 (1989), 1+.

[7] John Paul II, General Audience (22 February 1989), 1+.

perfection of the human species,"[8] and just as men rise encompassing their various statures, they will also rise with their sex as male or female. He explains, "And though there be difference of sex there will be no shame in seeing one another, since there will no lust to invite them to shameful deeds which are the cause of shame."[9] He continues:

> Christ never did and never will put aside the body which once for all he reassumed in his resurrection; according to Romans vi, 9: *Christ having risen again from the dead dies no more.* Therefore the saints also will live for ever with the bodies in which they rose again: and thus human bodies will remain after the end of the world.[10]

---

[8] *ST*, Supplement, q. 81, a. 3, ad 3.

[9] *ST*, Supplement, q. 81, a. 3, resp.

[10] Aquinas, *Quaestiones Disputatae*, q. 5, a. 10.

Augustine of Hippo says that those who argue, citing Paul's words, "there is no longer Jew or Greek, there is no longer slave or free, there is no longer male and female; for all of you are one in Christ Jesus (Gal 3:38)", and think that this means there is no "male or female" in the afterlife, are mistaking the meaning of this passage which regards barriers falling and abolished distinctions amongst believers—all are now "part of the same body" as joint heirs of divine inheritance.[11] This is in contrast with the prior Jewish perspective that only the sons of Abraham were God's chosen ones. In Christ, all are now one. Anthony Kelly, in a *Theological Studies* journal article, says that in the new-found belief and membership in the

---

[11] Augustine of Hippo, *The City of God, Books I-VII*, vol. 8, Foreword, I, ed. Hermigild Dressler, trans. Demetrius B. Zema and Gerald G. Walsh, Fathers of the Church (Washington, DC: Catholic University of America Press, 1950), 26.

body of Christ, "believers are offered a new sense of corporate coexistence: 'In that renewal there is no longer Greek and Jew, circumcised and uncircumcised, barbarian, Scythian, slave and free, but Christ is all and in all' (Col 3:11)."[12]

Joel Green calls our attention to an important point. He expresses that Paul insists that even though our bodies are the same yet transformed in the resurrection, "we should not imagine that our bodies are unimportant, then, or that what we do to our bodies or with our bodies is somehow unrelated to eternal life."[13] What we do with our bodies here on earth *matters* and is indicative of where we will spend our eternity. Not to be taken for granted, Green says that our bodily resurrection is a divine gift from God

---

[12] Anthony J. Kelly, "'The Body of Christ: Amen!': The Expanding Incarnation," *Theological Studies* 71 (2010), 809.

[13] Green, 173.

in which our new body is "not to be traded for the old," but will "subsume the old."[14] John Paul II concurs that the Pauline anthropology of the resurrection reveals that every man bears in himself the "image of Adam," but every man must also "bear in himself the image of Christ, the image of the Risen One."[15] Paul cautions:

> For you yourselves know very well that the day of the Lord will come like a thief in the night. When they say, 'There is peace and security', then sudden destruction will come upon them, as labour pains come upon a pregnant woman, and there will be no escape! But you, beloved, are not in darkness, for that day to

---

[14] Green, 175-176.

[15] Pope John Paul II, General Audience on Pauline Theology of the Body and the Resurrection of the Dead (3 February 1982), *L'Osservatore Romano* 721 (1982), 3.

surprise you like a thief; for you are all children of light and children of the day; we are not of the night or of darkness. So then, let us not fall asleep as others do, but let us keep awake and be sober; for those who sleep sleep at night, and those who are drunk get drunk at night. But since we belong to the day, let us be sober, and put on the breastplate of faith and love, and for a helmet the hope of salvation. For God has destined us not for wrath but for obtaining salvation through our Lord Jesus Christ, who died for us, so that whether we are awake or asleep we may live with him . . . . Do not quench the Spirit. Do not despise the words of prophets, but test everything; hold fast to what is good; abstain from every form of evil (1Thes 5:2-10; 19-22).

Aquinas answers many questions in his *Summa Theologiae* concerning all of man's various natural attributes and whether they will follow him into the resurrection. The following is his response to a question concerning one's hair and nails—indicative of his reasoned responses to such questions:

> It is written (Luke 21:18): *A hair of your head shall not perish.* Further, Hair and nails were given to man as an ornament. Now the bodies of men, especially of the elect, ought to rise again with all their adornment. Therefore they ought to rise again with the hair.
>
> And so among the parts of an animated body, some are directed to the accomplishment of the soul's operations, for instance the heart, liver, hand, foot; while others are directed to the safe-keeping of the other parts as leaves to cover fruit; and thus hair and nails are in man for the protection of other parts.
>
> Consequently, although they do not belong to the primary perfection of the human body, they belong to the second-

ary perfection; and since man will rise again with all the perfections of his nature, it follows that hair and nails will rise again in him. [16]

Aquinas sufficiently reasons that all will not be of the same stature in the afterlife either; for, he says, our "natural quantity" is not altered—so some men will be taller, some shorter, etc. Our "natural quantity," he says, is a result of each man's individual nature, and because it is a part of our very nature it will not change in the resurrection—this is barring any "error in the working of nature, resulting in the addition of something to or the subtraction of something from the aforesaid quantity." [17]

---

[16] *ST*, Supplement, q. 80, a. 2, sc, q. 80, a. 2, resp.

[17] *ST*, Supplement, q. 81, a. 2, sc, q. 81, a. 2, resp.

All of our senses will also be intact in the resurrection. In fact, they will be more perfect, says Aquinas: "A power conjoined to its act is more perfect than one not so conjoined. Now human nature in the blessed will be in its greatest perfection."[18] Also, because the glorified body is in complete submission to the will, the body will be able to be seen or not seen according to the act of the will, just as Christ was able to vanish from the disciples' sight in Luke 24:31 in Emmaus[19] and appear to walk through walls in John 20:19.

Theologian and bible scholar, Scott Hahn, says that when Jesus returns in his second coming to judge the living and the dead, he will "make his return 'in the same way'" he ascended into heaven—"visibly, tangibly, gloriously, wrapped in the heavenly cloud that had taken him to the right hand

---

[18] *ST*, Supplement, q. 82, a. 4, sc.

[19] *ST*, Supplement, q. 85, a. 3, sc.

of the Father (Acts 1:9; 2:32-33)." [20] We know this because it is written in the first chapter of Acts, when the two men dressed in white robes appear immediately upon Jesus' ascension saying, "'This Jesus, who has been taken up from you into heaven, will come in the same way as you saw him go into heaven' (Acts 1:10-11)." [21]

John Paul II in his theology of the body says that in the resurrection:

> Man will always be the same, just as he came forth from the hand of his Creator and Father. Christ says, 'They will take neither wife nor husband,' but he does not affirm that this man of the 'future world' will no longer be male and female as he was 'from the beginning'. It is thus

---

[20] Scott Hahn, "The Final Parousia," in *Catholic Bible Dictionary*, ed. Scott Hahn (New York: Doubleday, 2009), 675.

[21] Hahn (ed), *Catholic Bible Dictionary*, 675.

evident that the meaning of being, with respect to the body, male or female in the 'future world' should be sought outside of marriage and procreation, but there is no reason to seek it outside of that which (independently from the blessing of procreation) derives from the very mystery of creation and thereafter also forms the deepest structure of man's history on earth, given that this history was deeply co-penetrated by the mystery of redemption. [22]

In his original situation, man *is thus alone*, and at the same time, he *comes to be* as male and female: the unity of the two. In his solitude 'he reveals himself' to himself as person to 'reveal' at the same time the communion of persons in the unity of the two. In the one as well as the

---

[22] John Paul II, General Audience (13 January 1982), trans. Waldstein, 69:3, p. 398.

other state, the human being constitutes himself as image and likeness of God. From the beginning, man *is* also a body among bodies and in the unity of the two, he *comes to be* as male and female, discovering the 'spousal' meaning of his body in the measure of his being a personal subject . . . Yet, *the original* and fundamental *meaning of being a body*, as also of being, as a body, male and female—that is, precisely that 'spousal' meaning—is *united to the fact that man is created as a person and is called to a life 'in communione personarum'* . . . That 'spousal' meaning of being a body will, therefore, be realized as a *meaning that is perfectly personal and communitarian at the same time.*[23]

In 'this world'—*it is difficult to construct a fully adequate image* of the 'future

---

[23] John Paul II, 69:4, p. 399.

world.' Nevertheless, at the same time, there is no doubt that with the help of Christ's words at least a certain approximation to this image is possible and reachable. [24]

---

[24] John Paul II, 69:7, p. 400.

CHAPTER 4
GENDER, SIN, AND "THE FALL"

MALE AND FEMALE: IN COMMUNION

In John Paul II's *Man and Woman He Created Them: A Theology of the Body*, the saint focuses our attention on God's words in Genesis 2:24, "A man will leave his father and his mother and unite with his wife, and the two will be one flesh," saying that this has "from the beginning constituted the condition and relation of masculinity and femininity."[1] He goes on to say:

> Given that the words of Genesis were the threshold, as it were, of the whole theology of the body—a threshold on which Christ based himself in his teaching

---

[1] John Paul II, General Audience (2 December 1981), trans. Waldstein, 66:4, p. 388-389.

about marriage and its indissolubility—
one must admit that his words reported
by the Synoptics are like a new threshold
of this integral truth about man, which
we find again in the revealed Word of
God. It is indispensable for us to dwell
on this threshold if we wish our theology
of the body—and also our Christian
'spirituality of the body'—to be able to
use it as a complete image. [2]

He continues,

It is a sign that the body, whose end is
not death, tends toward glorification; already by this very fact it is, I would say, a
testimony among men that anticipates
the future resurrection. [3]

---

[2] John Paul II, General Audience (13 January
1982), trans. Waldstein, 69:8, p. 401.

[3] John Paul II, General Audience (24 March
1982), trans. Waldstein, 75:1, p. 419.

Pope Francis adds that after God creates the first man, Adam, He realizes that man alone by himself "is not good,"—he lacks "something to reach his fullness." [4] What is missing, says Francis, is communion and reciprocity for man; thus, God creates woman, a helpmate made specifically for him, as seen in Genesis 2:18.

Francis says that when man finds woman in the Bible he has to leave something behind (his father and his mother) in order to find her fully, emphasizing, "It's beautiful! This means setting out on a new path. Man is everything for woman and woman is everything for man." [5] He maintains that it is not man or woman alone who are the image of God, but man and woman as a couple

---

[4] Pope Francis. General Audience (22 April 2015), in *Audiences of Pope Francis, 2013-2015 (English)* (Vatican City: Libreria Editrice Vaticana, 2016), Verbum: Logos Bible Software.

[5] Pope Francis, Ibid.

who image God.[6] He says their very difference is for their own sakes to be able to share
in relationship with each other and for the
purposes of procreation.[7] Francis says to really know one's self, and to develop as a human being, one needs the reciprocity that
comes from the male/female relationship.
When this is lacking, he says, we see the
consequences. [8] Citing his concerns, he
states:

> I ask myself, if the so-called gender theory
> is not, at the same time, an expression of
> frustration and resignation, which seeks
> to cancel out sexual difference because it
> no longer knows how to confront it. Yes,
> we risk taking a step backwards. The re-

---

[6] Pope Francis. General Audience (15 April
2015), in *Audiences of Pope Francis, 2013-2015
(English)* (Vatican City: Libreria Editrice Vaticana, 2016), Verbum: Logos Bible Software.

[7] Pope Francis, Ibid.

[8] Pope Francis, Ibid.

moval of difference in fact creates a problem not a solution.

God entrusted the earth to the alliance between man and woman: its failure deprives the earth of warmth and darkens the sky of hope. The signs are already worrisome, and we see them. I would like to indicate, among many others, two points that I believe call for urgent attention.

The first . . . we must do far more to advance women, if we want to give more strength to the reciprocity between man and woman.

We have not yet understood in depth what the feminine genius can give us, what woman can give to society and also to us. Maybe women see things in a way that complements the thoughts of men.

A second reflection concerns the topic of man and woman created in the image of God. I wonder if the crisis of collective trust in God, which does us so much

harm, and makes us pale with resigna-
tion, incredulity and cynicism, is not also
connected to the crisis of the alliance between man and woman. In fact the biblical account . . . tells us in fact that the
communion with God is reflected in the
communion of the human couple and the
loss of trust in the heavenly Father gener-
ates division and conflict between man
and woman.

The great responsibility of the
Church, of all believers, and first of all of
believing families . . . impels people to rediscover the beauty of the creative design
that also inscribes the image of God in the
alliance between man and woman. The
earth is filled with harmony and trust
when the alliance between man and
woman is lived properly.[9]

---

[9] Pope Francis, Ibid.

MALE AND FEMALE: GENDER PHENOMENOLOGY AND COMPLEMENTARITY

Francis affirms that it is complementarity that each gender provides to the other by way of one's masculine and feminine gifts and attributes, which exist to enrich one's relationship. "Without the mutual enrichment of this relationship—in thought and in action, in affection and in work, as well as in faith—the two cannot even understand the depth of what it means to be man and woman."[10] He also insists society "must return marriage and the family to the place of honour!"[11]

John Paul II, in his epistle on the dignity and vocation of women, *Mulieris dignitatem*, recognizes a philosophically significant sex-

---

[10] Pope Francis, Ibid.

[11] Francis, General Audience (22 April 2015), Verbum: Logos Bible Software.

ual differentiation gender phenomenology, which Lawrence P. Porter, author of the article, "Gender in Theology: The Example of John Paul II's *Mulieris dignitatem*," points out. John Paul II says that it is one's male or female gender phenomenology—in existence since the start of humanity—that conditions one's freedom by its irrevocable gender-specific gifting, qualities, and Godly given call and vocation as a man or a woman.[12] Porter says John Paul identifies the "psycho-physical structure of women," who possess a biological and psychological nature open and welcoming to life, and compares it with the "psycho-physical structure" of men, which necessitates an "existential independence from his own generativity" for the pur-

---

[12] Lawrence B. Porter, "Gender in Theology: The Example of John Paul II's *Mulieris dignitatem*," *Gregorianum* 77, no. 1 (1996), 98, 111.

poses of his calling and possible priestly religious vocation.[13]

With regard to Christ and his priests who do not enter into the sacrament of marriage, Sara Butler, contributor to *Women, Sex & the Church: A Case for Catholic Teaching*, explains that "Christ's male sex, and therefore the priest's, contribute to the sacramental symbolism," of Christ's love for his Church and his willingness to sacrifice for her on the Cross—correlating it with man's love for a woman.[14] She says that Christ, Head of the Church, is male on account of God's plan and willing of sexual difference from the very beginning, not because men are superior to women, but because of the order established by God enabling the

---

[13] Porter, 111-114.

[14] Sara Butler, "Embodied Ecclesiology: Church Teaching on the Priesthood," in *Women, Sex and the Church: A Case for Catholic Teaching*, ed. Erika Bachiochi (Boston: Pauline Books & Media, 2010), 158.

(male) priest to be "a living sign" of Christ's spousal relationship to His Church.[15]

The U.S. Bishops' Committees on Marriage and Family and Domestic Policy affirm the Roman Catholic Church's definition of marriage as an "exclusive and lifelong union between one man and one woman joined as husband and wife in an intimate partnership of life and love."[16] The Church distinguishes two equal and inseparable aspects of marriage: the unitive aspect and the procreative aspect.[17] The Bishops' Committees express that marriage is vitally important for the continuation of the human race, but it also exists for the aid of individual human development, familial prosperity, and the peace, dignity, and stability within society.[18]

---

[15] Butler, 158-159.

[16] Suprenant and Gray, 121.

[17] *CCC, 2366.*

[18] Suprenant and Gray, 121.

Heinrich Denzinger concurs that the dynamic of male/female companionship produces the "primary form of interpersonal communion," that aids one in living and developing his potential. [19] Nicholas Tonti-Filippini notes that because the Church regards the person as one unity—body and soul *together* constituting the human person, gender is not to be regarded as "merely a psychological or social concept, but one grounded in the physical reality of the body." [20]

William May, author of the essay, "'Male and Female He Created Them': Catechesis on Human Sexuality and Sexual Ethics," acknowledges that male/female sexual complementarity, in particular, "signifies that the male person is intended by God as a 'gift' to the female person and vice versa," and that man and woman, through marriage and the

---

[19] Denzinger, *Compendium*, 940.

[20] Tonti-Filippini, 93-94.

begetting of children, image God even more fully.[21] Scott Stiegemeyer reveals that Satan vehemently attacks the conjugal union between man and woman because this union "is God's most powerful image in the world. Unable to strike God himself, the enemy strikes God's image!"[22]

The Church specifies that the gift of a child comes not from outside of the couple, but rather from "the very heart" of mutuality between them as "fruit and fulfillment" of their married love,[23] mirroring the mystery of the Trinitarian love between the Father, Son, and Holy Spirit. Leon Suprenant and Philip Gray denote that while some hus-

---

[21] William E. May, "'Male and Female He Created Them': Catechesis on Human Sexuality and Sexual Ethics," in *The Great Life: Essays on Doctrine and Holiness*, ed. Michael J. Aquilina and Kenneth M. Ogorek (Steubenville, OH: Emmaus Road Publishing, 2005), 138.

[22] Stiegemeyer, 47.

[23] *CCC, 2366.*

bands and wives are physically unable to bear children, they still nonetheless "complete one another through the expression of mutual love" and by means of their reciprocative marital relations.[24] Brian Bransfield, author of *The Human Person: According to John Paul II*, remarks that a couple unable to bear children has "not deliberately deprived the conjugal act of its procreative potential. They still engage and receive all the blessings of the gift of self in love. Their witness of love, often lived in the shadow of the cross, is a unique contribution to the meaning of marriage."[25]

Jennifer Roback Morse, another contributor to *Women, Sex & the Church*, says the Church recognizes that our individual male and female genders enlighten us to our limi-

---

[24] Suprenant and Gray, 120.

[25] J. Brian Bransfield, *The Human Person: According to John Paul II* (Boston, MA: Pauline Books & Media, 2010), 110-111.

tations and interdependence upon one another.[26] By ourselves, we cannot bring forth
new life. The fact that man and woman cooperate in bringing new life into the world,
and that their children are extremely dependent upon them for their survival and
care for many years, attests to marriage being an admittedly cooperative endeavor between man and woman.[27] She says that Ca-
tholicism sees "difference" as a good thing
amongst the sexes—not a bad thing—and
that it is precisely this "difference" that necessitates our interpersonal communion
helping us rise in our highest perfection as
human beings.[28]

---

[26] Jennifer Roback Morse, "The Liberation of
Lifelong Love: Church Teaching on Marriage,"
in *Women, Sex & the Church: A Case for Catholic Teaching*, ed. Erika Bachiochi (Boston: Pauline Books & Media, 2010), 93.

[27] Morse, 93-94.

[28] Morse, 93.

Garcia also remarks that the different strengths of men and women, when combined, produce helpful, constructive results in achieving goals.[29] Regarding the care of children, she asserts, "nothing succeeds like a mother and father who both work hard at preserving their marital friendship and meeting the needs of their children," maintaining that "sociological evidence is overwhelming on this point."[30] She cites differences men and women bring to the table on the familial home front and explains that although there are variations family to family, by and large, women provide children with understanding, love, support, and encouragement, while men provide physical strength and focus more on "making the family secure, both physically and financially."[31] These differences, Garcia attests, make

---

[29] Garcia, 24.

[30] Garcia, 24.

[31] Garcia, 25.

men and women grateful for each other's unique gender-based gifts and characteristics such that they purposely *seek* one another out in relationships because of their complementarity. [32]

"THE FALL" AND ITS CONSEQUENCES FOR GENDER

In Genesis 2:16-17, God commands Adam not to eat from the tree of "the knowledge of good and evil," telling him that the day he eats of it he "shall die." Man is told that he can eat from every other tree in the garden, except this one tree. In Genesis 3:6-7, the woman, Eve, takes fruit from this forbidden tree, eats it, and gives some to her husband, Adam, who also eats it. The moment they partake of this fruit the eyes of Adam and Eve are opened, and they recognize that they are "naked" (Gn 3:7). Upon

---

[32] Garcia, 25.

hearing the Lord God in the garden after committing this sin, "the man and his wife" hide from God (Gn 3:8). Because of their disobedience, the world changes henceforth for mankind, as God expressly delineates in Genesis 3:8-19. Living in a paradisiacal land and experience prior to The Fall, man now finds himself in a land laden with "thorns and thistles" which he is to till by the sweat of his brow until death (Gn 3:18-19). This newfound condition man finds himself in comes about because of his sin and is considered "the fall of mankind," or more succinctly: "The Fall."

The *Catechism of the Catholic Church* says that this fallen world which "we notice so painfully does not stem from the *nature* of man and woman, nor from the nature of their relations, but from *sin*," as it is a rupture of the original experience of communion between man and woman.[33] Christopher

---

[33] *CCC*, 1607.

West, author of *Theology of the Body Explained*, says that gender difference bears the brunt of blame for man's sins since The Fall, but he brings to light John Paul II's declaration that man is not really ashamed after The Fall because of his gendered *nakedness* but because of his new *concupiscence* to sin and his lust.[34] "In other words," West explains, "man may attribute shame to the body and to gender difference, but this is almost always an excuse not to contend with the disorder of his own lustful heart."[35]

Man and woman, after The Fall, tend towards self-gratification and the use of one another as objects,[36] lacking the persistent, selfless, other-directed centered love they possessed prior to The Fall. Interestingly,

---

[34] Christopher West, *Theology of the Body Explained*, rev. ed. (Boston, MA: Pauline Books & Media, 2007), 183.

[35] West, 183.

[36] West, 183.

denotes Christopher West, this new embodied awareness not only ruptures man's 'from the beginning' relationship with God and the woman, it ruptures his relationship with the rest of Creation.[37] Continuing to relay John Paul's theology of the body, West says:

> Now, however, even the earth resists man and his task of 'tilling the soil.' The ground itself is 'cursed' because of him (see Gen 3:17). Here we see that man's experience of his own gendered embodiment affects questions of ecology and questions of a society's work and economic structures. These issues are inseparable from sexuality, marriage, and family life. We must first reclaim the true meaning of these if we are to establish harmonious relationships with the environment, within the workplace,

---

[37] West, 186.

within culture at large, and between na-
tions.[38]

Both Leon Suprenant and Philip Gray
say that neither two men nor two women
can legitimately marry one another, regardless of legislation seeming to justify such
marriages in courts of law, because of the
truth that lies within us—namely our *natural reason* which informs us otherwise, and
because we have the benefit of Christ's divine Revelation.[39] Christ confirms marriage
as a sacrament by performing his first public
miracle at the wedding feast at Cana (Jn 2:1-
11). Husband and wife, say Suprenant and
Gray, "are called to imitate and participate
in the nuptial union of Christ and His bride,
the Church."[40] Man and woman *naturally*
complement one another biologically and

---

[38] West, 186.

[39] Suprenant and Gray, 119.

[40] Suprenant and Gray, 119.

socially, they express, in contrast with homosexual relationships, which are *unnatural*, lack complementarity, and which present an "illusory and vain attempt" at the "communal love of the Holy Trinity" God envisions for man and woman.[41] God created sexual difference and complementarity, says Scott Stiegemeyer, and everyone has a 'true sex' regardless of whether one is able to distinguish it or not due to one's physiology or confusion, saying that God ultimately knows one's true gender.[42] Brian Bransfield, says:

> Only two things that are truly different can be united. Two things that are the same form a set, but cannot form a unity. Two things that are the same are aligned extrinsically. But they have no substantial difference in their very na-

---

[41] Suprenant and Gray, 119-120.

[42] Stiegemeyer, 47.

ture that can give them a reciprocity. Unity presupposes difference . . . . The sexual difference takes place in and through the body in all its masculine and feminine fullness, and is the matrix for the total gift of self.[43]

Going even further, allowing homosexual marriages, say Suprenant and Gray, paves the way for legitimizing the norm of polygamous marriages in courts of law, further eroding societal morality, there being "no logical argument against" such marriages when abandonment of the monogamous man/woman standard of marriage prevails.[44]

HOPE FOR GENDERED MANKIND

The importance of gender to the human soul is not without meaning in the next or

---

[43] Bransfield, 107.

[44] Suprenant and Gray, 120-121.

the present life. Together, man and woman reflect the divine Trinity. Together, man and woman complete one another with a complementarity and a reciprocity that either gender, by itself, cannot attain alone. God has necessitated that man and woman enter into communion with one another to meet one another's needs and to perpetuate the human race. There is hope, however, for mankind as the Church expresses that God is always ready to offer his healing and mercy to those who come asking for His forgiveness of their sins. Without God's help, says the Church, "man and woman cannot achieve the union of their lives for which God created them 'in the beginning'."[45]

---

[45] *CCC*, 1608.

CHAPTER 5
THE ASSUMPTION AND GENDER
IN THE AFTERLIFE

THE ASSUMPTION

On November 1, 1950, Pope Pius XII promulgated the Apostolic Constitution *Munificentissimus Deus* attesting the divinely revealed dogma "that the Immaculate Mother of God, the ever Virgin Mary, having completed the course of her earthly life, was assumed body and soul into heavenly glory."[1] To clarify, due to the merits Mary received from Christ via his atoning death and resurrection, and in anticipation of her assent to the angel Gabriel to become the Mother of the Savior, Mary is Immaculately conceived in the womb of her mother, Anne. Free from sin due to her Immaculate Con-

---

[1] Denzinger, 809.

ception, the Virgin is therefore worthy of the distinct privilege of being assumed body and soul into Heaven at the appointed time by God. The notion of Assumption is not new; authors Peter Kreeft and Ronald Tacelli say the Jewish people understand Enoch, Elijah, and possibly even Moses, to have been assumed into Heaven. [2]

The Second Vatican Council's dogmatic constitution, *Lumen gentium*, speaks of the Assumption of the Mother of Christ:

> Finally, the Immaculate Virgin, preserved free from all guilt of original sin[1], on the completion of her earthly sojourn, was taken up body and soul into heavenly glory[2] and exalted by the Lord as Queen of the universe, that she might be the more fully conformed to her Son,

---

[2] Kreeft and Tacelli, *Handbook*, 190.

the Lord of lords [*cf. Rev 19:16*] and the conqueror of sin and death.[3]

John Paul II explains that the Church recognizes Mary as the "woman clothed with the sun" in Revelation 12:1 and "the woman" who struggles with Satan/the serpent/the dragon in the same biblical chapter.[4] Mary is the first to be redeemed and the "great portent" appearing as a sign, he says, because she never acquiesces "*to the spirit of lies*".[5] Because of this, John Paul maintains that Mary "has the maternal power *to guide man, in the Spirit of Truth* through this age of great lies in which he lives."[6]

---

[3] Denzinger, 906.

[4] Pope John Paul II, General Audience on The Future of the World and of Mankind Lies in the Mystery of Mary's Assumption (15 August 1984), *L'Osservatore Romano* 849 (1984), 3.

[5] Pope John Paul II, Ibid.

[6] Pope John Paul II, Ibid.

Again, in *Munificentissimus Deus*, the Church proclaims Mary:

> . . . immaculate in her conception, a most perfect virgin in her divine motherhood, the noble associate of the Divine Redeemer, who has won a complete triumph over sin and its consequences, finally obtained, as the supreme culmination of her privileges, that she should be preserved free from the corruption of the tomb and that, like her own Son, having overcome death, she might be taken up body and soul to the glory of heaven where, as Queen, she sits in splendor at the right hand of her Son, the immortal King of the Ages [*cf. 1 Tim 1:17*] . . . .[7]

---

[7] Denzinger, *Compendium*, 809.

THE ASSUMPTION:
FURTHER EVIDENCE OF BODILY
RESURRECTION, INCLUDING GENDER

The dogma of the Assumption of the Virgin Mary provides another powerful meditation on the realization of one's own bodily resurrection and glory in the afterlife. The Venerable Archbishop Fulton J. Sheen acknowledges that Mary, by her Assumption, "becomes the first human person to realize the historical destiny of the faithful as members of Christ's Mystical Body, beyond time, beyond death, and beyond judgment."[8] The most compelling reason for accepting Mary's Assumption and retention of gender in the afterlife, says Donald Calloway, is that:

---

[8] Fulton J. Sheen, *The World's First Love: Mary, Mother of God*, 2nd ed. (San Francisco: Ignatius Press, 1996), 140.

. . . the dogmatic formulations about the Virgin Mary both affirm and complement what John Paul II taught about the human body. As a matter of fact, it can be stated with certainty that if these two areas—John Paul II's theology of the body and the Church's Marian dogmas—were in theological discord, there would exist a serious problem due to the fact that 'to speak of Mary,' as Cardinal Ratzinger states, 'is to touch on the *nexus mysteriorum*—the inner interwovenness of the [Christian] mysteries.[9]

Calloway continues, "Mary is at the heart of all the teachings of the Church because she is at the heart of Christianity. Every teaching about Mary will affirm, must affirm, a teaching about Christ and His Church."[10] Mary's only desire is to point us

---

[9] Calloway (ed), 62.

[10] Calloway (ed), 62.

to her Son, Jesus, and all honors that he affords his Mother are means by which he reveals to mankind our attainable future.[11]

The Assumption of Mary, articulates Calloway, teaches that after one's earthly life is over, "we will continue to be body-persons, either in heaven or in hell . . . we do not shed our bodies," for God is maker of everything—including our bodies—and declares them "good."[12] John Paul II affirms, says Calloway, that the Assumption teaches us about the goodness of our bodies by expressing that "every human body" is called to be an instrument of holiness to one day be able to share a life of glory with God in the eternal kingdom.[13] Heinrich Denzinger in his compendium concurs, "Man is not allowed to despise his bodily life," but to regard the body as "good and honorable" since

---

[11] Calloway (ed), 63.

[12] Calloway (ed), 61-62.

[13] Calloway (ed), 62.

God made him and wishes for him to return to Him—body and soul—in Heaven. [14]

Mary, says Calloway, freely accepts the gift of becoming the mother of the Savior in her *femininity* and as a *woman, but* he says, if she had rebelled against her feminine body, "*we* would be in a very different situation today." [15] Calloway emphasizes that Mary shows us how to accept our bodies, including our gender. He says that Mary sees her body not as an obstacle to be overcome but as a gift, explaining that she delights in her body and in her femininity because it is *through* her femininity that she is able to be the *Theotokos* [Mother of God]. [16] The Virgin, states Calloway, "plays a crucial role in theology in helping us to better understand that Christian teachings concerning the

---

[14] Denzinger, *Compendium*, 941.

[15] Calloway (ed), 55-56.

[16] Calloway (ed), 56.

body are not abstract philosophical ideas, but real, concrete embodied realities."[17]

Fulton Sheen gets to the heart of the Assumption saying that what this dogma actually affirms is *love*. He cites Aquinas who states that one of love's greatest effects is *ecstasy*. In ecstasy, Sheen says, "one is 'lifted out of his body'" somewhat resembling levitating off the ground—a feat some saints accomplish due to their intense love of God.[18] Sheen uses an analogy: love is like fire, which burns upward seeking to unite with its beloved object of desire.[19] For the Virgin Mary, the object of her desire following her Son's death, Resurrection, and Ascension is reunification with him. Sheen also describes a corollary, "If the distant moon moves all the surging tides of earth, then the love of Mary for Jesus and the love of Jesus for Mary

---

[17] Calloway (ed), 63.

[18] Sheen, 133.

[19] Sheen, 133.

should result in such an ecstasy as 'to lift her out of this world'."[20] We are all called to this ecstasy of love with our Savior. Our weakened bodies and wills that refuse the love of God and rebel against Him keep our bodies bound to the earth.[21]

John Paul II reveals that the Assumption of Mary manifests man's final destiny and reconfirms God's divine plan for man's salvation.[22] *Lumen gentium* concurs:

> In the interim, just as the Mother of Jesus, glorified in body and soul in heaven, is the image and beginning of the Church as she is to be perfected in the world to come, so too does she shine forth on earth, until the day of the Lord shall come [*cf. 2 Pet 3:10*], as a sign of

---

[20] Sheen, 134.

[21] Sheen, 134.

[22] John Paul II, General Audience (15 August 1984), 3.

sure hope and solace to the people of God during its sojourn on earth. [23]

As denotes the *Catechism*, the Assumption of Mary anticipates "the resurrection of other Christians," [24] saying, "In giving birth you kept your virginity; in your dormition you did not leave the world, O Mother of God, but were joined to the source of Life. You conceived the living God and, by your prayers, will deliver our souls from death." [25]

CHURCH APPROVED MARIAN APPARITIONS: FURTHER EVIDENCE OF MARY'S ASSUMPTION AND RETENTION OF GENDER IN THE AFTERLIFE

The Catholic Church, at times, recognizes private revelations given to men, women,

---

[23] Denzinger, *Compendium*, 908.

[24] *CCC*, 966.

[25] *CCC*, 966.

and children. These private revelations in no way surpass or correct Christ's Revelation but only aid one in living Christ's Revelation "more fully . . . in a certain period of history."[26] Approved apparitions undergo intense scrutiny and investigation by the Church and are deemed to hold nothing contrary to faith or morals. Very brief samplings of some of these apparitions are cited below to demonstrate how various visionaries throughout the centuries report seeing the Virgin Mary, who is assumed in Heaven, and who returns presenting herself to some privileged souls upon the earth.

The most famous of Marian apparitions takes place in Fatima, Portugal, in the year 1917. In Fatima, Mary appears to three shepherd children—Lucia, Francisco, and Jacinta, ages 9, 8, and 6. Lucia attests they witness, "a Lady of all white, more brilliant than the sun dispensing light, clearer and

---

[26] *CCC*, 67.

more intense than a crystal cup full of crystalline water penetrated by the rays of the most glaring sun."[27] Mary speaks to the children several times, and they describe her presence as "more peaceful" and "comforting" than prior visions with an angel they had seen. Jacinta says she is, "such a pretty Lady!"[28]

Another well-known apparition of Mary takes place in 1531 in Guadalupe, Mexico, to a 57-year-old man, Juan Diego. One morning, as Juan nears the top of a hill, he hears strange music and then a "woman's voice calling above the music,"[29] recounts Catherine Odell, author of *Those Who Saw Her: Apparitions of Mary*. According to Odell, Juan drops to his knees and smiles upon see-

---

[27] Catherine M. Odell, *Those Who Saw Her: Apparitions of Mary*, updated and rev. ed. (Huntington, IN: Our Sunday Visitor Publishing, 2010), 139.

[28] Odell, 140-141.

[29] Odell, 40.

ing a strikingly beautiful young woman who radiates intense light, beckoning to him.[30] This "woman" speaks to Juan several times informing him thusly, "You must know and be very certain in your heart, my son, that I am truly the perpetual and perfect Virgin Mary, holy Mother of the True God through whom everything lives, the Creator and Master of Heaven and Earth."[31]

In 1830, the Virgin appears to St. Catherine Labouré in her convent chapel. As Catherine recounts, "I heard the rustling of a silken robe coming from the side of the sanctuary. The 'Lady' bowed before the tabernacle, and then she seated herself" in a chair, and, says Catherine, "I rushed forward and knelt before the Blessed Virgin with my hands on her knees. I cannot express what I felt, but I am sure that this was the happiest

---

[30] Odell, 40.

[31] Odell, 40.

moment of my life."[32] Another time when Catherine sees the Blessed Virgin, she discloses that each of her fingers "exhibited beautiful precious jewels of differing sizes and colors."[33]

When the Virgin appears in 1846 to 11-year-old Maximin and 14-year-old Melanie in La Salette, France, she appears as if in a globe. "She was seated," relays Odell from the children's account, "bent forward, with her face buried in her hands and her elbows resting on her knees. It was the very picture of a woman weeping as through she had suffered the greatest loss of her life."[34] When the woman stands, the two children are amazed at her beauty. She is wearing a long white dress, a translucent headdress with crown, a roses-trimmed shawl, yellow apron, white slippers affixed with pearls and gold

---

[32] Odell, 69.

[33] Odell, 72.

[34] Odell, 83.

buckles, and she has a cross around her neck.[35]

In Banneux, Belgium, in 1933, the Blessed Virgin Mary comes as "an unbelievably beautiful woman," to eleven-year-old Mariette Beco, dressed in a "flowing white gown and white veil, with a brilliant blue sash" possessing a rosary in her hand.[36] In Kibeho, Rwanda, beginning in 1981, sixteen-year-old Alphonsine sees "an incredibly beautiful Lady" with skin that is "not really white like we see her in pictures . . . but she was of an incomparable beauty," wearing a white veil, white dress, and no shoes.[37]

And in another quite famous apparition that takes place in Knock, Ireland in 1879, Mary Byrne sees three figures appearing to be the Blessed Virgin, St Joseph, and St John. Of her vision of Mary, she recalls:

---

[35] Odell, 84.

[36] Odell, 176.

[37] Odell, 226.

The Virgin stood erect, with eyes raised to heaven, her hands elevated to the shoulders or bosom; she wore a large cloak of a white color, hanging in full folds and somewhat loosely gathered around her shoulders and fastened to the neck; she wore a crown on the head—rather a large crown—and it [the cloak] appeared to me somewhat yellower than the dress or robes worn by Our Blessed Lady.[38]

St. Joseph is bent towards Mary, in Mary Byrne's vision, while St John is "dressed in Mass vestments, wearing a bishop's miter on his head and holding a book in his left hand," with his right hand "raised in blessing."[39]

These apparitions demonstrate that the Virgin Mary returns to earth from Heaven

---

[38] Odell, 129.

[39] Odell, 129.

in her respective human likeness and with her female gendered body, much like Her Son did between his Resurrection and Ascension. In each of Mary's apparitions, she is cited wearing distinctly feminine articles and accessories—a shawl, rings, necklace, gown or dress, apron, veil, pearls, etc. As heavenly beings, Jesus and Mary can come to earth dressed any way they like. They choose, however, to come dressed in common articles relative to their genders—wanting to be seen, understood, recognized, and remembered as holy beings in complete possession of their distinctive gendered bodies.

CHAPTER 6
THE CONCLUDING LINK

The Catholic Church recognizes, along with its saints John Paul II and Thomas Aquinas, that gender is indeed an eternal aspect of the human soul. Without one's gendered body, which God creates as "good" and which constitutes part of the completeness of the human person, one's soul cannot rest in the afterlife. Man is a body/soul composite. His personhood will not exist whole until reunited with his body in the resurrection. Aquinas reminds us that until our souls and bodies are reunified, perfect beatitude cannot be obtained.

John Paul II's theology of the body and Aquinas' reasoning regarding the body and soul in the afterlife give us a clearer understanding of the essential characteristics necessary to our humanness in the afterlife. Donald Calloway states,

Christianity is an embodied religion, and without a proper understanding of the body, Christianity cannot be fully understood. This is precisely why John Paul II sought to give to the world a theological anthropology that presents to the world an objective teaching on the human body.[1]

One's soul and body are inseparably linked. Gender in a human being necessitates the soul so a person can *know* God. A human soul necessitates gender so that a person can *love* God. One's gender helps the soul to love God because in our flesh we are weak and in need of God. We also have need of one another's gender complementarity in order to complete in our humanness the image of God more fully.

Man and woman's bodies are made to be complementary. They are made to bring

---

[1] Calloway (ed), 63.

forth life by the generation of children. Through procreation we are joined in one human family. This generation of life transmitted by a man and woman reflects the love between the three persons of the Divine Trinity. Masculinity and femininity are distinctly given gifts to the soul indicating one's vocation and path to eternal life. Our gendered differences aid us in loving one another because it is *precisely* because of our differences that we need one another—physically, psychologically, socially, and emotionally. Our gendered nature pushes us to be in communion with one another just as we need to be in communion with our God.

Science reveals that even men's and women's brains are different. We think differently, we process information differently, we process emotions differently, and we communicate differently. Thomas Aquinas says that each man possesses a different "quantity" with the differences between the sexes in existence *for* the other, filling the gap. Our gendered differences consist of gifts, strengths, and weaknesses designed to *complement* one another and as *cause of our desire and need* to seek one another out to be in complementary reciprocal relationship with.

Gender is fixed. It is not malleable. Men and women *together* reflect the image of God. John Paul II identifies that our differences provide the basis for our equal dignity. Our bodies will be changed in quality in the resurrection, but not in substance. Being male or female gendered individuals in the resurrection will be constituted differently than our life as gendered beings here on earth. In the afterlife, gender will no longer be for procreation, as the time for man and woman to "subdue the earth" will be accomplished. We will, however, retain our masculinity and femininity and our distinctive male and female attributes, characteristics, and individualities. The Assumption of the

Virgin Mary and her approved apparitions and visitations upon the earth, as well, provide us with further evidence of what our own bodily resurrection will look like.

Our bodies will rise in the general resurrection, as did Christ's in his Resurrection. We will rise as *human* beings, not as angels who are entirely spirit beings. Our *nature* as human beings will not change. Our nature will be perfect as God created and intends it to be. Heaven demands the perfection of our personhood; therefore, everything in man in his corporeal body and spiritual soul must be perfect in Heaven. In Heaven, man's body and soul will exist in perfect harmony.

Though man is a fallen creature, in Heaven his body will be made perfect, and imperfections will no longer exist. Whether one rises to Heaven, or falls to Hell, one's gender will be retained in both soul and body. Man may become confused, nature itself may have produced an aberration in his body veiling his true gender, but God is not perplexed. In any case in which human science may still be unable to determine one's gender, one can rest assured that in the life to come the "peace of God, which surpasses all understanding" (Phil 4:7) will come to him and make him whole.

What matters here in this life is conforming one's life to Christ—in happiness, in sorrow, and in all of life's mysteries, as a true, loving disciple. For Jesus says:

> If you love me, you will keep my commandments. And I will ask the Father, and he will give you another Advocate, to be with you for ever. This is the Spirit of truth, whom the world cannot receive, because it neither sees him nor knows him. You know him because he abides with you, and he will be in you (John 14:15).

By seeking truth through science, philosophy, theology, the magisterial teachings of the Catholic Church, man's natural reason, and via the great gifts of holy wisdom bestowed upon the Church in her pronounced saints—particularly John Paul II the Great and Thomas Aquinas, doctor of the Church, the truth about gender and its eternal link to the human soul has been discovered and revealed.

BIBLIOGRAPHY

Adolphe, Jane and Robert L. Fastiggi. "Gender (in International Law)." In *New Catholic Encyclopedia Supplement 2012-2013: Ethics and Philosophy*, vol. 2, ed. Robert L. Fastiggi, 612-614. Detroit: Gale, 2013.

Anderson, Mary Jo and Robin Bernhoft. *Male and Female HE MADE THEM: Questions and Answers about Marriage and Same-Sex Unions*. San Diego: Catholic Answers, 2005.

Aquinas, Thomas. *Quaestiones Disputatae de Potentia Dei: On the Power of God*. Trans. English Dominican Fathers. At Dominican House of Studies Priory of the Immaculate Conception, www.dhspriory.org.

Augustine of Hippo. *City of God, Books I-VII*. Vol. 8. Ed. Hermigild Dressler.

Trans. Demetrius B. Zema and Gerald G. Walsh. Fathers of the Church. Washington, DC: Catholic University of America Press, 1950.

Bernard of Clairvaux. *Bernard of Clairvaux: Selected Works*. Ed. John Farina. Trans. G. R. Evans. New York: Paulist Press, 1987.

Bransfield, J. Brian. *The Human Person: According to John Paul II*. Boston, MA: Pauline Books & Media, 2010.

Butler, Sara. "Embodied Ecclesiology: Church Teaching on the Priesthood." In *Women, Sex & the Church: A Case for Catholic Teaching*, ed. Erika Bachiochi, 158-159. Boston: Pauline Books & Media, 2010.

Butler, Sara. "Sex or Gender?" *First Things* 154 (2005): 43-46.

Calloway, Donald, ed. *The Virgin Mary and Theology of the Body*. Stockbridge, MA: Marian Press, 2005.

Case, Susan S. and Angela J. Oetama-Paul. "Brain Biology and Gendered Discourse." *Applied Psychology: An International Review* 64, no. 2 (2015): 338-378.

Catechism of the Catholic Church. 2nd ed. Washington, DC: United States Catholic Conference, 2000.

Denzinger, Heinrich. *Compendium of Creeds, Definitions, and Declarations on Matters of Faith and Morals.* Ed. Peter Hünermann. San Francisco: Ignatius Press, 2012.

Gadenz, Pablo. "The Church as the Family of God." In *Catholic for a Reason: Scripture and the Mystery of the Family of God*, ed. Scott Hahn and Leon J. Suprenant, Jr., 81-82. Steubenville, OH: Emmaus Road Publishing, 1998.

Garcia, Laura L. "Authentic Freedom and Equality in Difference." In *Women, Sex & the Church: A Case for Catholic Teaching*, ed. Erika Bachiochi, 16, 22, 23. Boston: Pauline Books & Media, 2010.

Green, Joel B. *Body, Soul, and Human Life: The Nature of Humanity in the Bible*. Studies in Theological Interpretation, eds. Craig G. Bartholomew and Christopher R. Seitz. Grand Rapids, MI: Baker Academic, 2008.

Hahn, Scott. "The Final Parousia." In *Catholic Bible Dictionary*, ed. Scott Hahn, 675. New York: Doubleday, 2009.

Heilig, Christoph. "Resurrection and the Eoundation [*sic*] of Christian Behaviour: Paul and Origen in Dialogue." *Colloquium* 46, no. 2 (2014): 196.

The Holy Bible: New Revised Standard Version, Catholic Edition. Washington, DC: National Council of Churches of Christ, 1993. Verbum: Logos Bible Software.

John Paul II. Encyclical on the Gospel of Life *Evangelium vitae* (25 March 1995). Boston: Pauline Books & Media, 1995.

John Paul II. *Man and Woman He Created Them: A Theology of the Body*. Trans.

Michael   Waldstein.   Boston: Pauline
Books & Media, 2006.

Kelly, Anthony J. " 'The Body of Christ:
Amen!': The Expanding Incarnation."
Theological Studies 71, (2010): 792-816.

Kreeft, Peter. *Everything You Ever Wanted
to Know about Heaven . . . but Never
Dreamed of Asking.* First Edition. San
Francisco: Ignatius Press, 1990.

Kreeft, Peter J., and Ronald K. Tacelli.
Handbook of Catholic Apologetics. San
Francisco: Ignatius Press, 2009.

May, William E. "'Male and Female He Cre-
ated Them': Catechesis on Human Sexu-
ality and Sexual Ethics," in *The Great
Life: Essays on Doctrine and Holiness*, ed.
Michael J. Aquilina and Kenneth M.
Ogorek (Steubenville, OH: Emmaus
Road Publishing, 2005), 183.

McHugh. "Surgical Sex." *First Things* 147
(2004): 34-38.

McInerny, Ralph. *St. Thomas Aquinas.* Notre Dame, IN: University of Notre Dame Press, 1982.

Merriam-Webster. "Gender." at Encyclopedia Britannica Academic Edition, 1 August 2017, at www.academic.eb.com.

Morse, Jennifer Roback. "The Liberation of Lifelong Love: Church Teaching on Marriage." In *Women, Sex & the Church: A Case for Catholic Teaching,* ed. Erika Bachiochi, 93-94. Boston: Pauline Books & Media, 2010.

Odell, Catherine M. *Those Who Saw Her: Apparitions of Mary.* Updated and rev. ed. Huntington, IN: Our Sunday Visitor, 2010.

Ott, Ludwig. *Fundamentals of Catholic Dogma.* Ed. James Canon Bastible. Trans. Patrick Lynch. Charlotte, NC: TAN Books, 1974.

Oxford English Dictionary. "Gender." at Oxford University Press, 6 November 2017, at www.oed.com.

Pope Francis. *Audiences of Pope Francis, 2013-2015 (English).* Vatican City: Libreria Editrice Vaticana, 2016. Verbum: Logos Bible Software.

Pope John Paul II. General Audience on Characteristics of the Apparitions of the Risen Christ (22 February 1989). *L'Osservatore Romano* 1078 (1989): 1.

Pope John Paul II. General Audience on The Future of the World and of Mankind Lies in the Mystery of Mary's Assumption (15 August 1984). *L'Osservatore Romano* 849 (1984): 3.

Pope John Paul II. General Audience on Our Bodies Will Share in the Resurrection (4 November 1998). *L'Osservatore Romano* 1566 (1998): 11.

Pope John Paul II. General Audience on Pauline Theology of the Body and the Resurrection of the Dead (3 February

1982). *L'Osservatore Romano* 721 (1982): 3.

Porter, Lawrence B. "Gender in Theology: The Example of John Paul II's *Mulieris dignitatem.*" *Gregorianum* 77, no. 1 (1996): 97-131.

Sheen, Fulton J. *The World's First Love: Mary, Mother of God.* 2nd ed. San Francisco: Ignatius Press, 1996.

Siegmund, Marianne J. "Gender: Philosophy of." In *New Catholic Encyclopedia Supplement 2012-2013: Ethics and Philosophy*, vol. 2, ed. Robert L. Fastiggi, 614. Detroit: Gale, 2013.

Stiegemeyer, Scott. "How Do You Know Whether You are a Man or a Woman?" *Concordia Theological Quarterly* 79, no. 1-2 (2015): 19-48.

Suprenant, Leon J., Jr., and Philip C. L. Gray. *Faith Facts: Answers to Catholic Questions.* Vol. 1. Steubenville, HO: Emmaus Road Publishing, 1999.

Tabor, Clarence Wilbur. "Gender." In *Tabor's Cyclopedic Medical Dictionary*, ed. Clayton L. Thomas. Philadelphia: F. A. Davis Company, 1985.

Thomas Aquinas. *Summa Theologica*. Trans. Fathers of the English Dominican Province. London: Burns Oates & Washbourne, 1921.

Tonti-Filippini, Nicholas. "Sex Reassignment and Catholic Schools." *The National Catholic Bioethics Quarterly* 12, no. 1 (2012): 85-97.

Wallace, William. *The Elements of Philosophy: A Compendium for Philosophers and Theologians*. 2nd ed. Eugene, OR: Wipf and Stock Publishers, 2011.

Ware, James. "Paul's Understanding of the Resurrection in 1 Corinthians 15:36-54." *Journal of Biblical Literature* 133, no. 4 (2014): 835.

West, Christopher. *Theology of the Body Explained*. Rev. ed. Boston, MA: Pauline Books & Media, 2007.

Willis, John R., ed. *The Teachings of the Church Fathers.* San Francisco: Ignatius Press, 2002.